Why Did I Do That?

How You Make Sense and Why There Is Hope:

An Introduction to Internal Family Systems (IFS)

Dorie Cameron, LICSW

ISBN - 0984052704
EAN-13 - 9780984052707
Printed in the United States of America

Published by Threshold Therapeutics Media
Natick, MA 01760
www.thresholdtherapeuticsmedia.com

Dedicated to

All parts in every being -
May they gently come home to Self

In full recognition of

Richard Schwartz, Ph. D.

- the man behind the big idea of this little book ~

The purpose of this book is to introduce
the basic tenets of Internal Family Systems (IFS).
Through simple pictures and just a few words,
one can easily grasp the concepts of this empowering,
inclusive and healing approach to psychotherapy.

Please recognize that the elegance and effectiveness
of the IFS model are more complex and life enhancing
than the simplicity of the images and words contained herein.

You are soul, spirit, pure consciousness, essence. You are Self.

You are wondrous,

...despite any messages you may have received to the contrary.

You ARE Self, and when you were born, you arrived with many parts.

Those parts were like seeds and each had the potential to become a helpful resource.

Self does not need to grow.

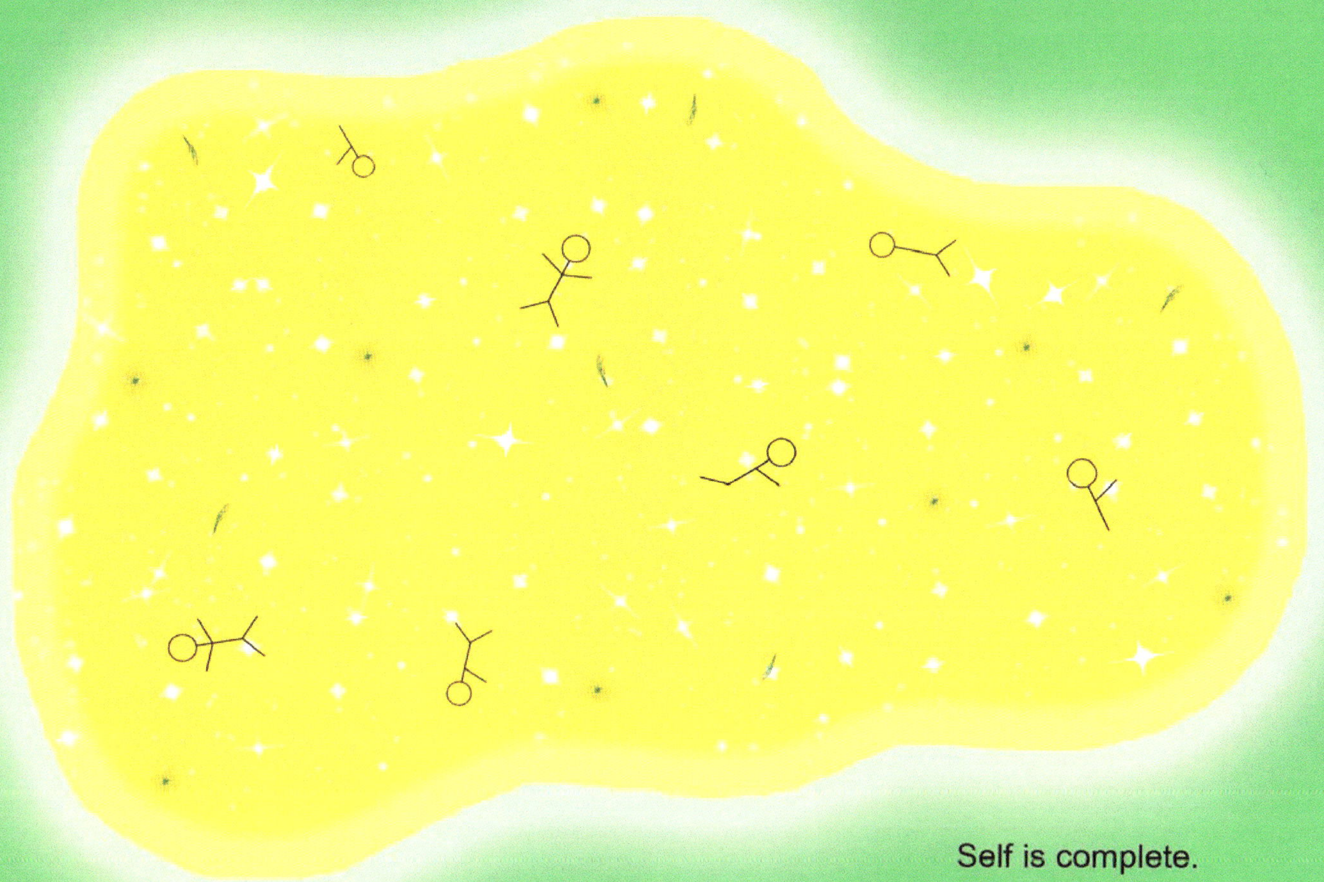

Self is complete.

Self and parts make up a system.

When the system is functioning harmoniously, it is in balance.

When the system is in balance,

When a system is in harmony, parts step forward to help. They get big, take up space and express themselves. When done,
they step back, allowing other
parts to come forward.

Parts develop complex interactions among themselves.

There is a lot of movement.

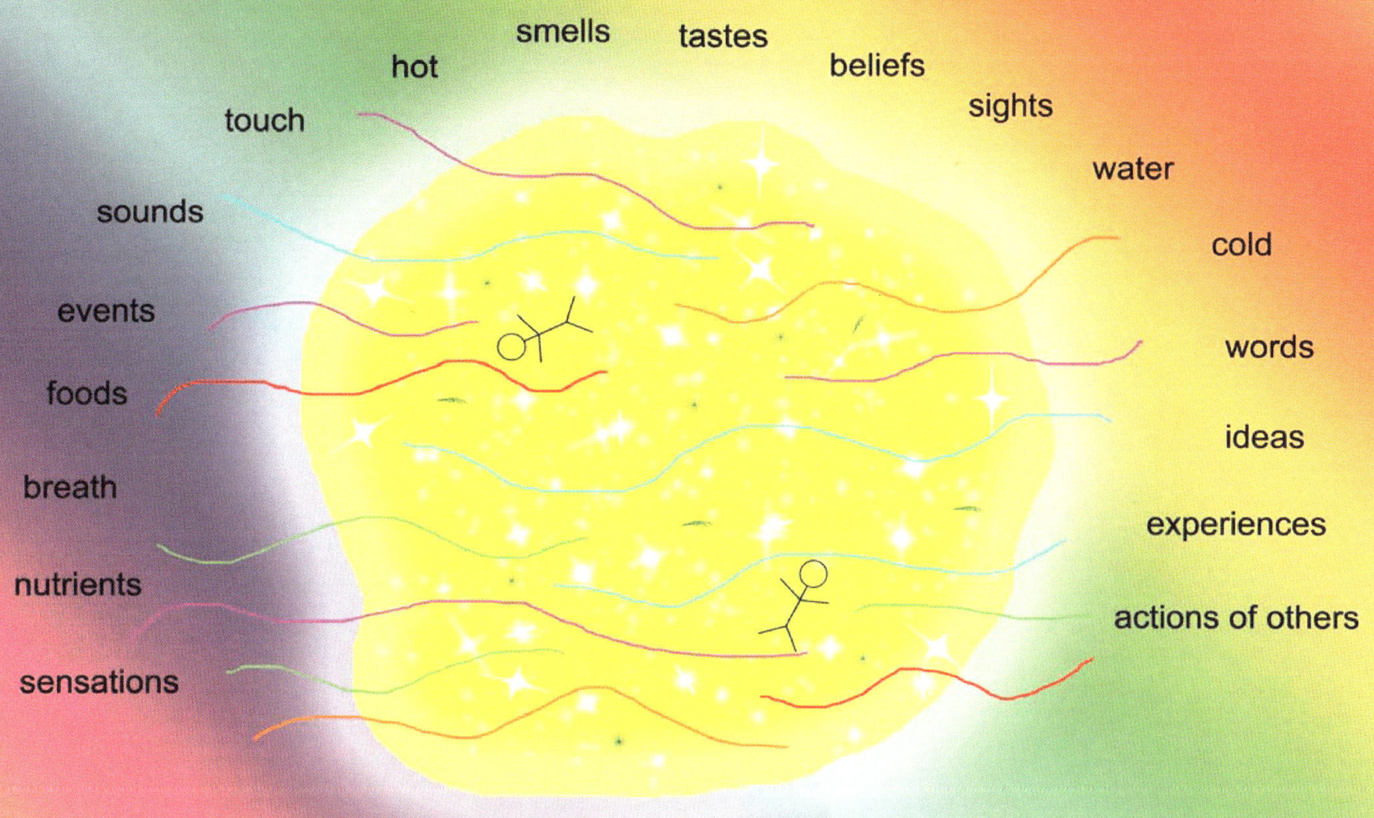

When life affects a balanced system, Self and parts respond.
smells
tastes
hot
beliefs
touch
sights
water
sounds
cold
events
words
foods
ideas
breath
experiences
nutrients
actions of others
sensations
This is natural!

Throughout life, all of us have experiences and hear messages.

Sometimes the messages can be neutral or positive and the system understands that it is not threatened.

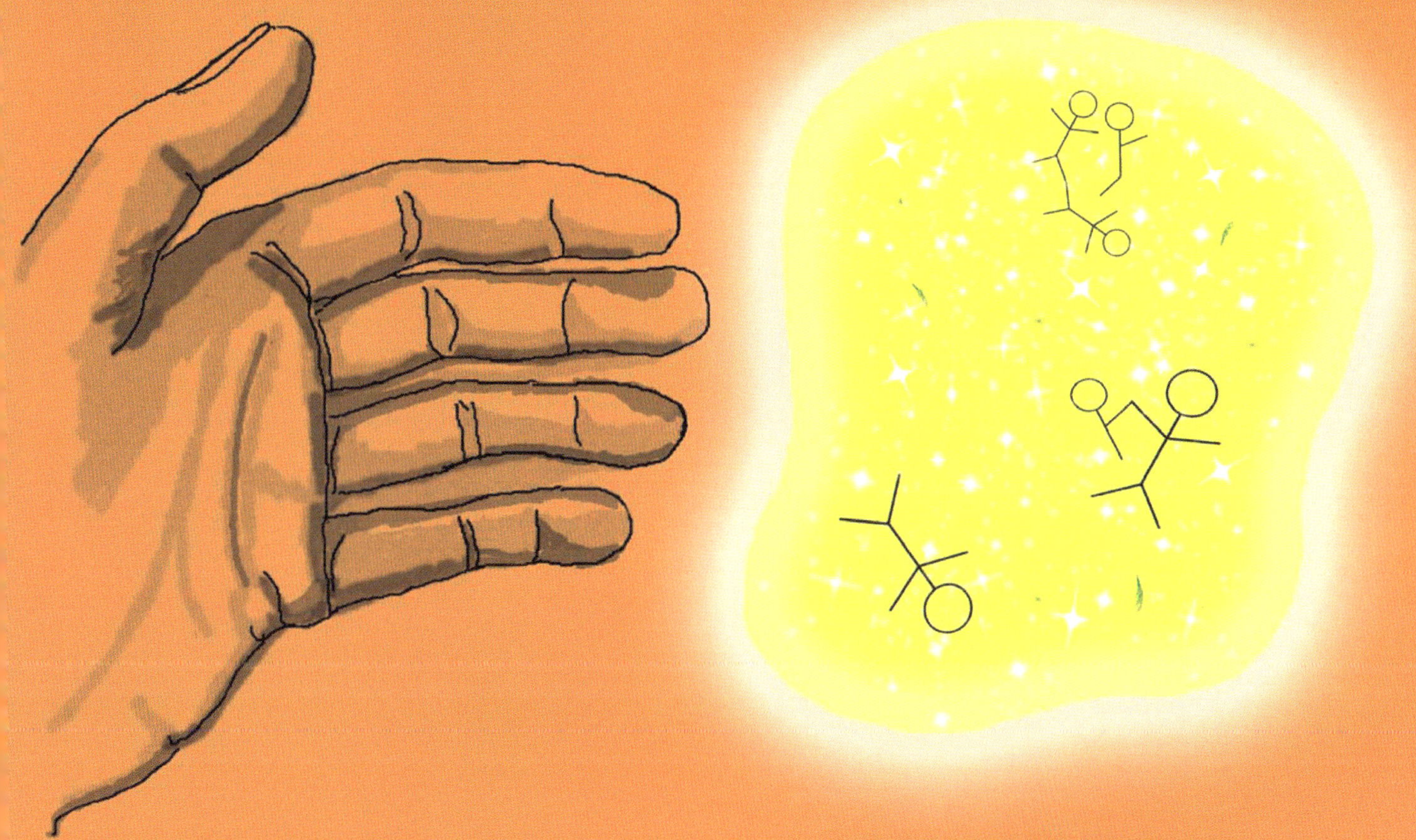

Sometimes an experience can be negative.

With luck, the system is met by another person's Self.

Then, parts are able to express themselves, receive compassion and feel connected.

Parts heal when they fully contact Self.

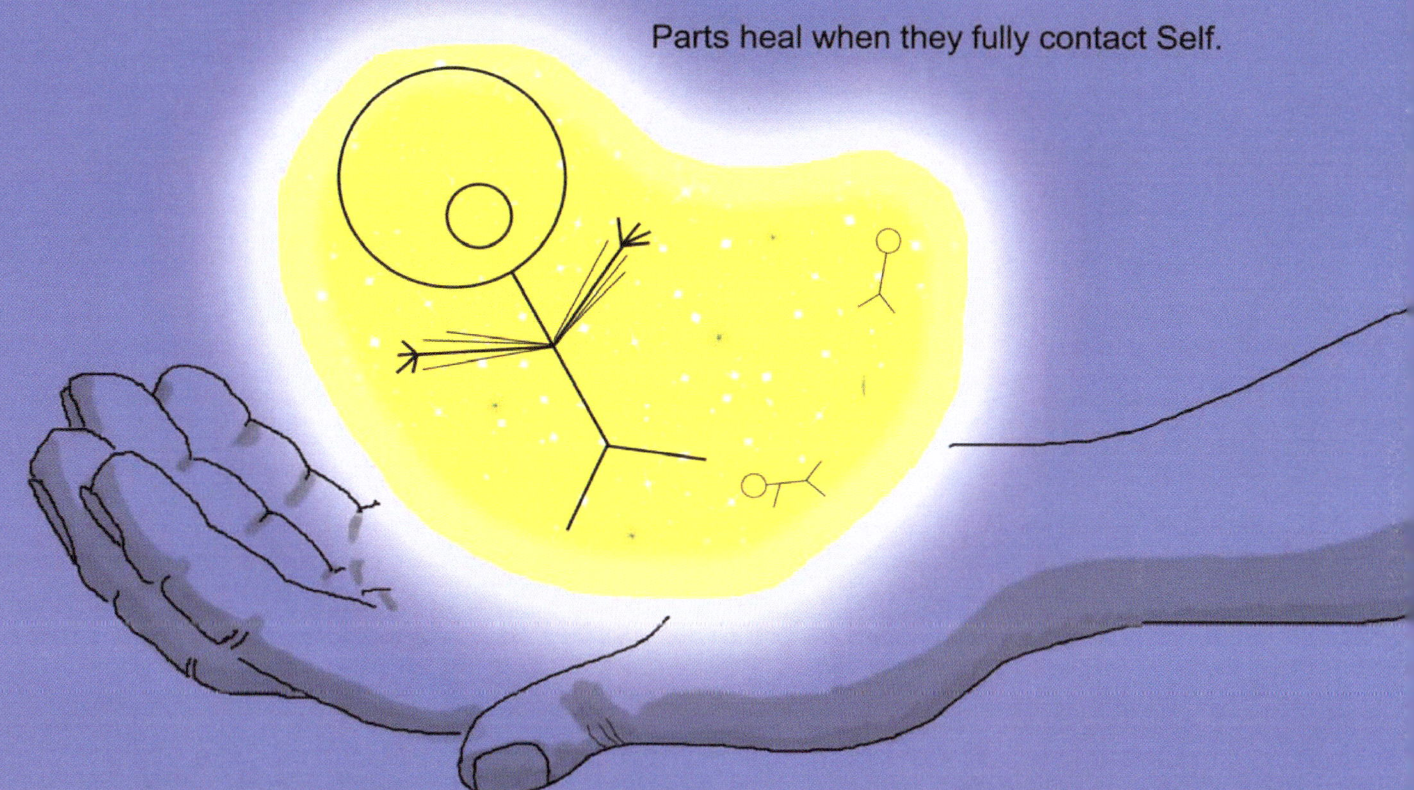

Within a system, parts can enjoy these qualities in the moment and over time.

11

Everyone knows that life includes a variety of experiences. While some are

comforting, thrilling, funny, enjoyable, peaceful, inspiring or hopeful

others can be

more challenging.

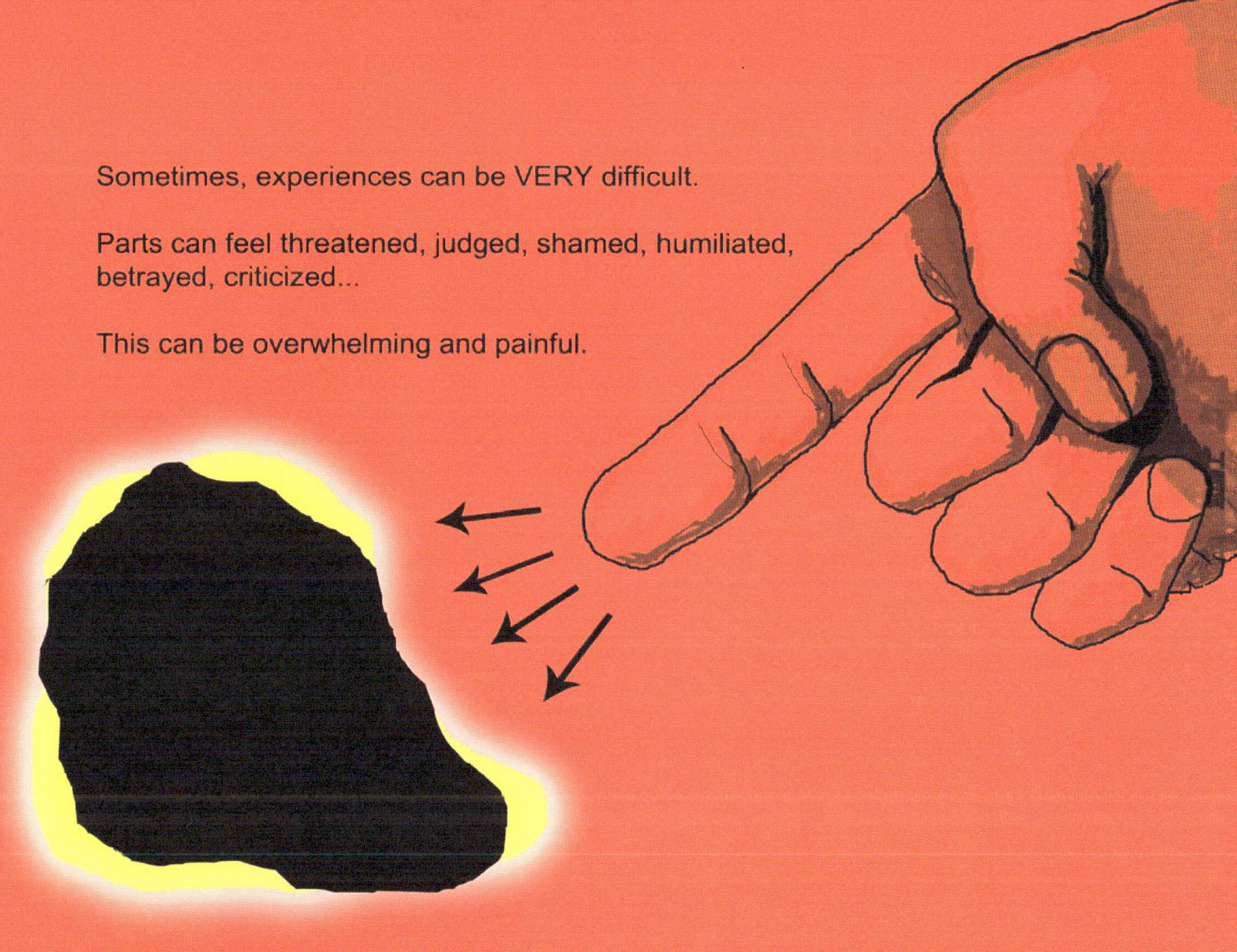
Sometimes, experiences can be VERY difficult.

Parts can feel threatened, judged, shamed, humiliated, betrayed, criticized...

This can be overwhelming and painful.

When parts get too overwhelmed, they can get confused and mistakenly assume they have no access to Self.
They feel it is up to them
to solve the problem,
deal with the challenge and

"fix it"...all on their own.

Parts DO have access to Self...

...but parts feel like they are alone.

One way parts respond and try to "fix it", is by making meanings or drawing conclusions.

A few examples are:

I can't handle life!

It's
all my
fault!

The world is not safe!

Making a mistake is
unacceptable!

A "bad" thing happened so I am unworthy of "good."

I am unlovable!

Another way parts respond is to restrict feelings that are perceived as too intense or dangerous.

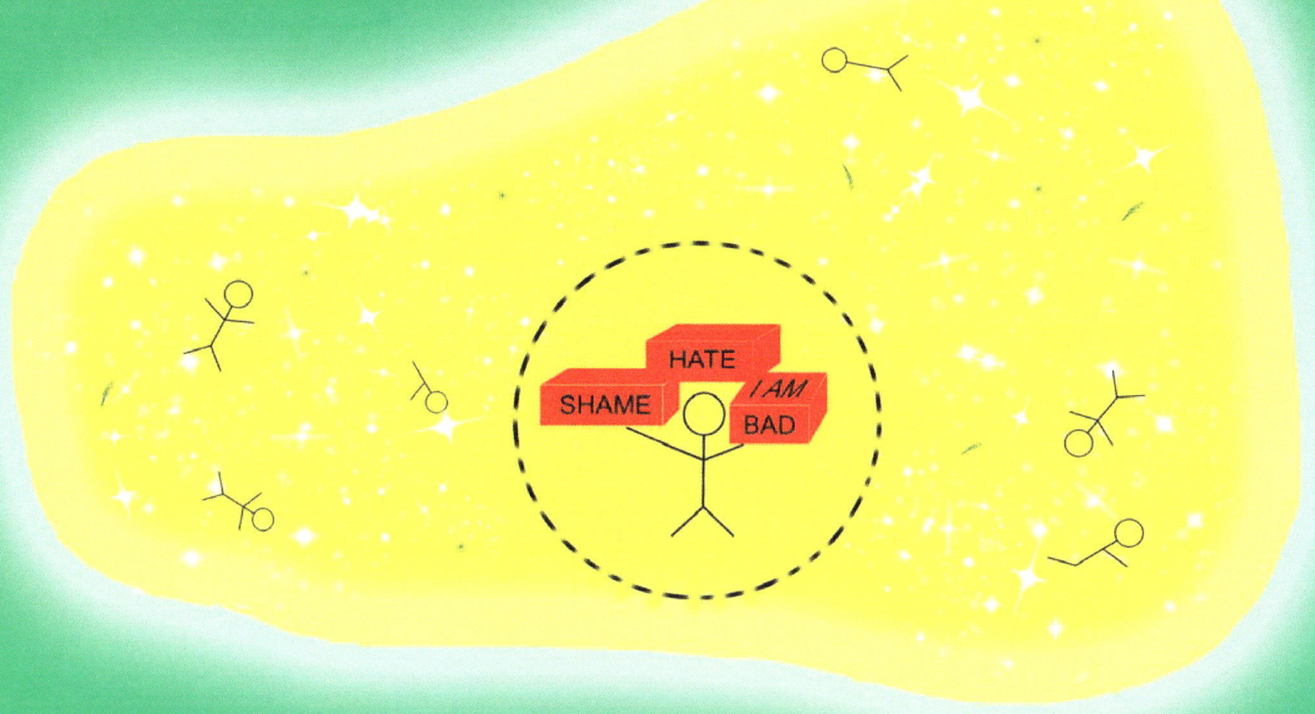

There is a "burdening" that occurs when meanings are made and feelings are not allowed. It is as if a part picks up a brick (a meaning, belief or feeling) and carries it around.

Bricks can be heavy.

Parts can feel protective of and/or bothered by the burdened one.

They respond in a variety of ways.

One option

is to hide

the part deep

down inside...

send it to a cave of sorts...

construct a barrier around it.

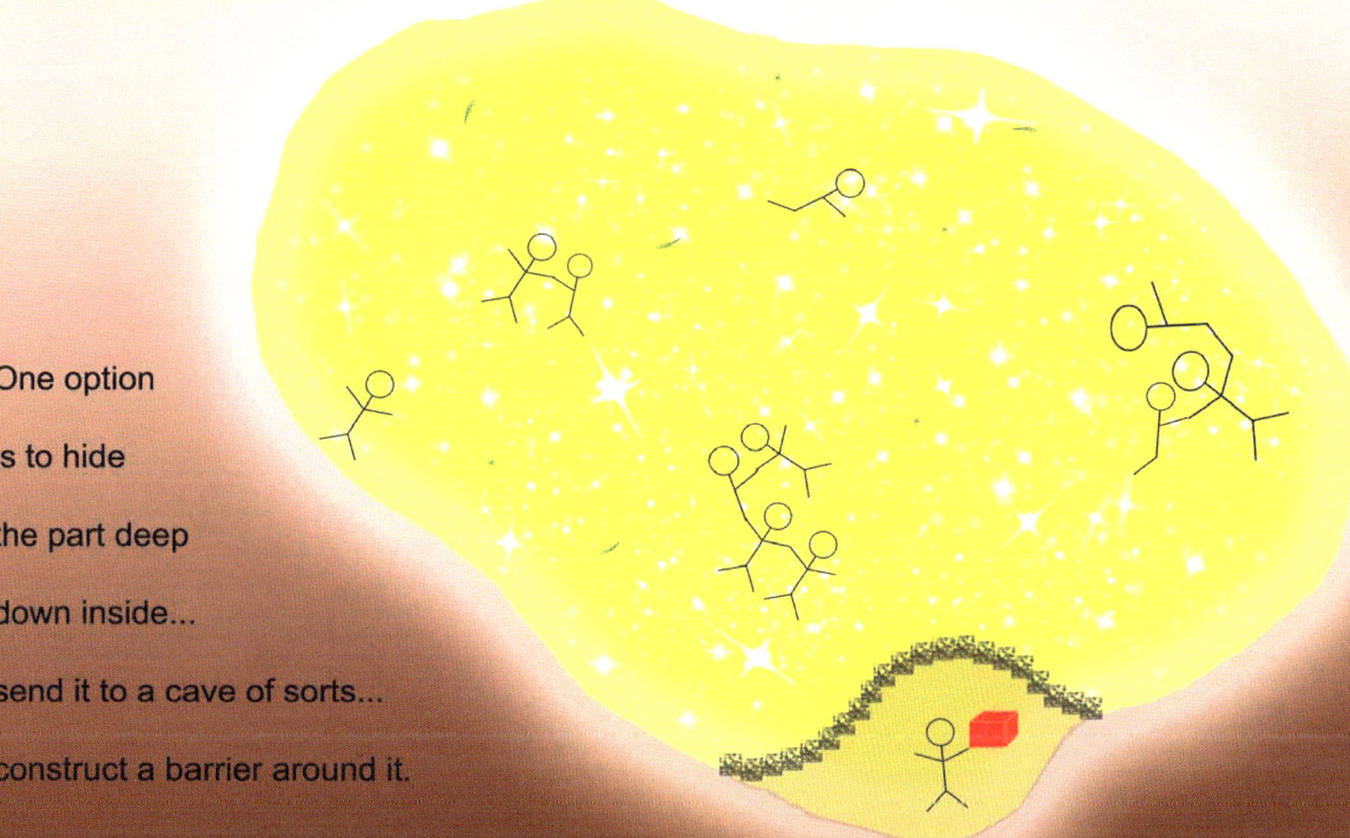

Another response is to freeze the part in time,

as if encasing it in ice.

The system can also try to eject the part.

Does it work to lock the part out or send it to the moon?

No! It is impossible to ever truly get rid of a part.

There is a force, a chord, a mystery, SOMETHING that keeps it attached to us...forever.

The purpose of these approaches is

PROTECTION

of the part, as well as the system.

The goal is to contain the part so it does not

get overwhelmed,
overwhelm the system or
express itself to others who might hurt that part again.

These three options—hiding, freezing or ejecting—

protect the part by keeping it separate.

We call these parts Exiles.

When a part is exiled, other parts recognize that they have a problem.

Parts know that the balance and harmony of the system have been compromised.

In order to restore at least a pseudo-balance to the system,

parts take action.

23

One part that loves to play and have fun, agrees to give up fun and put on a suit over its usual clothes.

represents its willingness to do whatever it takes to protect the Exile.

So, meet a Manager!

A Manager agrees to take on the task of trying to control what enters the system.

Its focus is to stop anything that may threaten the isolated state of the Exile.

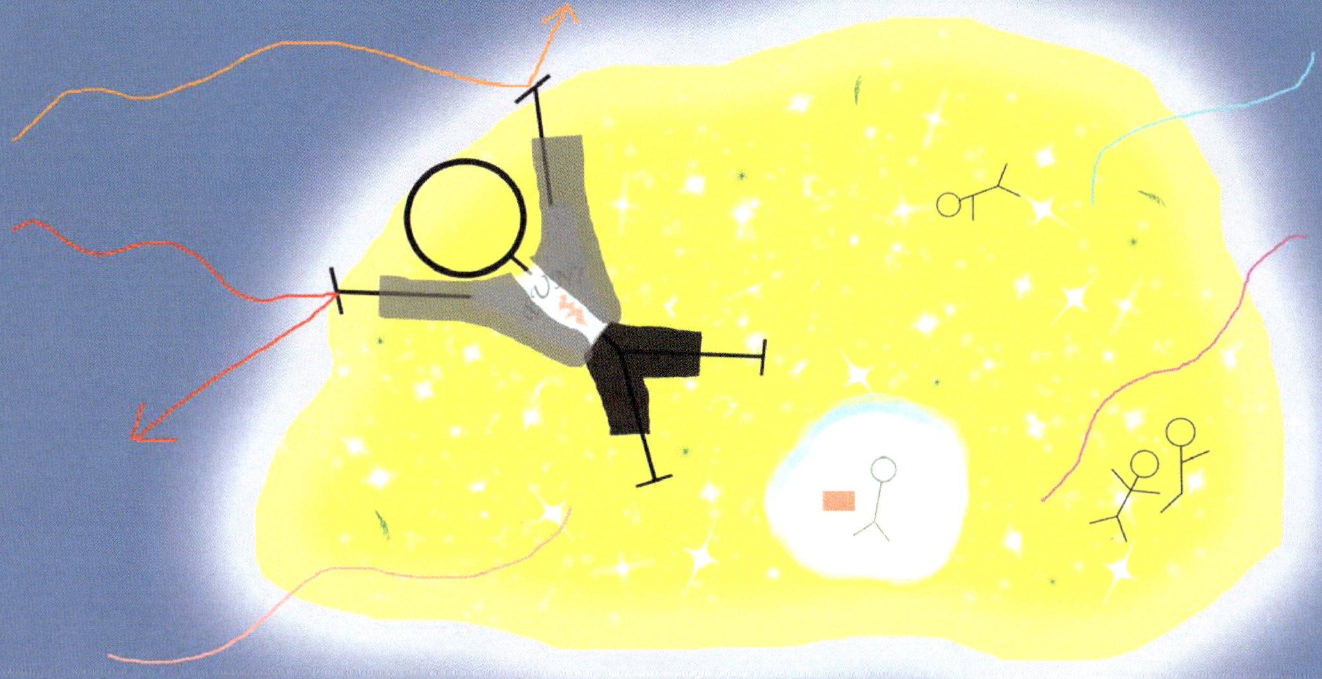

Often Managers feel burdened by their job.

Managers want to allow only the "right" things in and the "right" things ou[t].
They are concerned with day-to-day safety and appearances.

26

Sometimes Managers are unsuccessful and something "dangerous" slips past.

Fortunately,

the system has a back up plan.

Another part agrees to take on a different role:

Firefighter.

This part might prefer to swim and snorkel but, just as a Manager wears "Manager clothes," this part gives up swimming and agrees to put on Firefighter's gear.

Whenever a threat slips past the Manager,

the Firefighter grabs its equipment and

responds

QUICKLY,

STRONGLY

and

ACTIVELY

to the alarm!

The Firefighter will do ANYTHING
to protect the Exile!
It will have you
hit things
gamble
binge
go to sleep
diet excessively
smoke
get lost in daydreams
attack
drink too much
rage
overload on coffee
overwork
zone out watching TV
over-exercise
shop excessively
misuse sex

The Firefighter will
intensify actions
illegal drugs
stealing
violence
damaging relationships
self-destructive behaviors
until things are cooled, numbed, quenched, refrozen, re-barricaded.

30

Managers and Firefighters are doing their best to keep other parts safe.

Telling them to "just stop" is often futile.

Please know that Managers and Firefighters are very hard workers!
They work around the clock!
12
11
1
10
2
9
3
8
4
7
5
6
...year after year...

Remember there never were, nor are there now, any "bad" parts.

There are only parts in particular roles, doing particular jobs. Some parts work

in ways that appear misguided, oblivious, controlling, manipulative, scary, destructive, etc.

They may not like acting this way but they believe it is necessary.

33

So...what can you do?

34

You can enter into a journey of getting to know your parts...

...and your parts getting to know and trust YOU!

IT IS POSSIBLE FOR YOU

to develop kind and loving relationships with all your parts,

facilitate harmony among parts so the system can return to its natural balance,

assist parts to release their burdens,

help parts return to their preferred roles and

restore trust in your leadership.

All this can be done respectfully and gently.
All parts are welcome.

YOU ARE SELF!
YOU ARE WONDROUS!

To understand more read:

Introduction to the Internal Family Systems Model
and
You Are The One You Have Been Waiting For

by

Richard C. Schwartz, Ph.D., L.M.F.T.
Founder and Creator of the Internal Family Systems Model
President of the Center For Self Leadership

To find therapists, books, trainings and resources, visit
Center For Self Leadership at

www.selfleadership.org

Dorie Cameron, LICSW is a Licensed Clinical Social Worker
with over 20 years experience and additional
training in education, massage therapy and yoga.
She enjoys being in private practice in Framingham, MA and
feels honored to walk with people as they find their way to their truth.

I value IFS as a model for its capacity to meet every person
with deep respect and compassion.
I created this visual introduction so the IFS approach
could be accessible to as many people as possible.

May this book serve as a gentle invitation and offering of hope
for every person who has ever wondered
"Why did I do that?", "Am I truly bad?"
and
"What does it mean to 'love yourself'?"

Richard Schwartz, thank you for listening to and following your clients so carefully
and then forging a compassionate path upon which many walk and are
able to experience what it means to "love yourself".

Thank you for your presence
and love, sharing your gifts,
technological skills,
patient teaching,
kind and thoughtful
expressions, editing,
consultations,
conversations,
honest opinions,
inspirations,
generosity, visions,
a look, a word,
a tear, an ah-ha,
enthusiasm, a smile,
kindness, silence, company,
suggestions, gentle humor,
allowing, encouragement,
welcoming, belief in, patience,
openness, willingness, time,
letting go, courage, space,
educating, meeting, considering,
exploring, learning, listening,
responding, playing, clarity,
waiting, trusting and

THANK YOU

Rick, Kylie, Keaton,
DeeDee, John L, Carter, Thea,
Holly, Melody, Nick,
Karen, Phillips, Laura, Amy,
Betsy, JohnR,
Suzie, Tariq, Jaspar, Chloe,
Lee, Marcia, Pat M,
Julie G, Jon S,
Mona, Jeffry, Neil,
IFS trainers, assistants,
and participants who
I have been so fortunate
to learn with (and who
warmly received several
versions of this book),
Scott C, Meg B, Stephani M,
Katherine M, John B, Ted S, Marjorie F,
Elizabeth T, Lauren J-R, Lesley M,
Melissa F, my parents and theirs,
my clients who honor me with their
trust and awe me with their courage,
the earth and all the resources that went
into making this book (and, I believe,
benefit when we are Self-led), thank you!

...for sharing the journey!